Toe-rrific

A SIMPLE GUIDE TO CREATING
HEALTHY AND BEAUTIFUL FEET

Acknowledgements

We would like to show our appreciation to Valerie Moen and Priscilla Thomas for helping us to write up our never-ending ideas, Steve Shaw for all his patience, Alex Gore for everything he did to help us see the big picture, and to Oprah for encouraging us to help women "Live Their Best Lives".

Toe-rrific, A Simple Guide to Creating Healthy and Beautiful Feet.
Copyright © 2004 by Elena Prostova and Cathleen Shaw. All Rights Reserved.

Published by Happy Women Publishing Company, Ellenton, Florida.

64 pages
Library of Congress Cataloging-in-Publication Data is available upon request.
ISBN: 0-9745627-0-X
Library of Congress Number: 2003112572

Prostova, Elena
Shaw, Cathleen

Beauty, Healthcare
First Edition

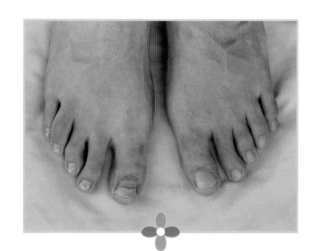

Alex

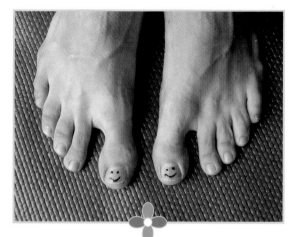

Steve

Vaska

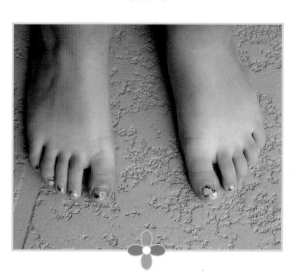

Maxx

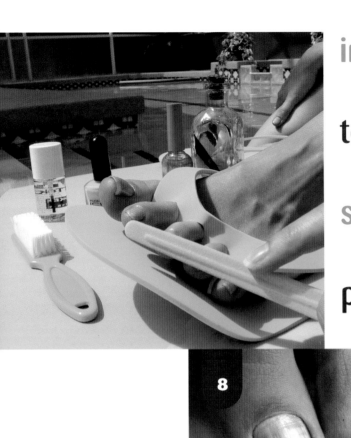

introduction

tools of the toes

step-by-step pedicure

painting 101

8

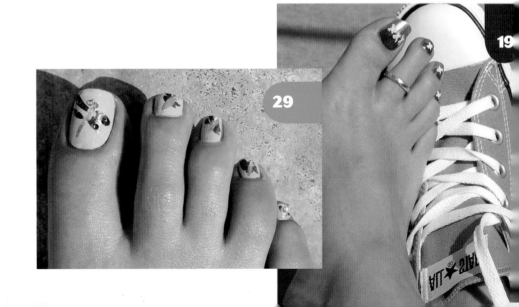

29

19

contents

nail designs

poor soles

resources

about us

order form

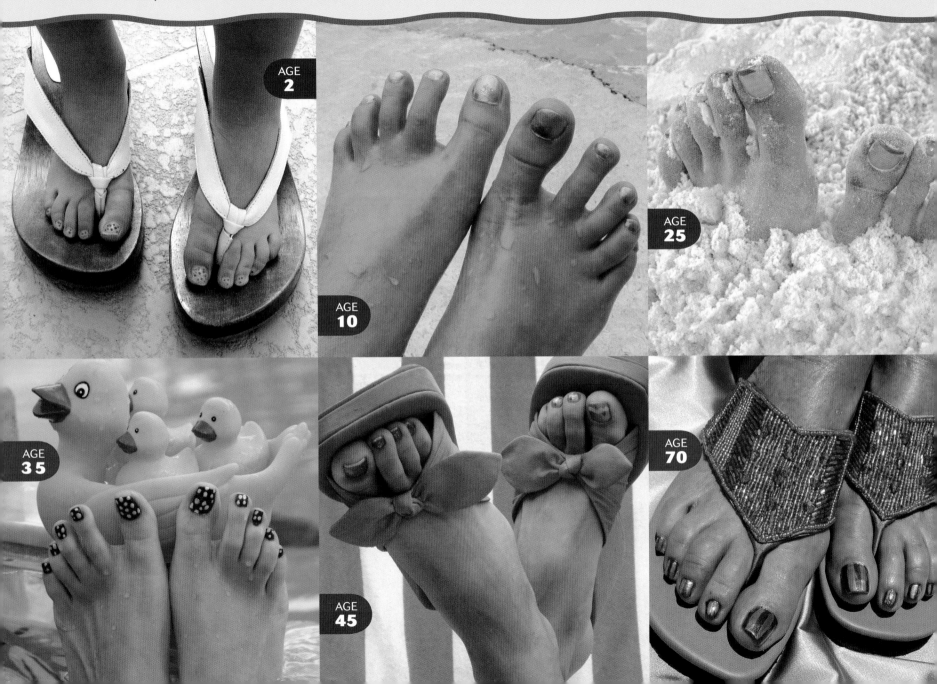

AT ANY AGE, IT'S WONDERFUL TO LEARN TO TAKE CARE OF YOUR TOES AND MAKE THEM BEAUTIFUL

AGE 2

AGE 10

AGE 25

AGE 35

AGE 45

AGE 70

LOVE YOUR TOES

So you are that special one holding this book... Have a look at your feet. Move your toes… Don't you see that they are smiling? They are happy because you noticed them, because you are going to take care of them and you will have lots of fun together.

You might not know it yet, but your toes are your best friends in the quest for beauty and uniqueness. Isn't it a worthy enough reason to love them? They are not as spoiled with attention as the other parts of your body! They are also more forgiving. Imperfections in applying polish will never affect the overall beautiful look of your toes. They are more up for experiments. Unlike your fingernails, they have no fear of bright colors or bold color combinations. Your toenails support your every fantasy, and at the same time, they are modest enough to hide in the socks or closed shoes when you don't feel like sharing them with the world.

HAVE FUN

We believe that everybody's feet are special and they can help us to feel special, too. By creating this book, we wanted to show how simple and exciting expressing your beautiful self could be. Taking care of your feet and experimenting with over 150 designs presented in this book is something fun to do by yourself and really fun to do with your friends during your own Toe-rrific group parties.

TENDER LOVING CARE

Making your toes feel beautiful starts with some relaxing pampering. In this book we introduce to you simple tools and beauty products for taking care of your feet. We show you how to get salon quality pedicure at home following a few easy steps. We also give you fun tips and easy to do ideas on feet maintenance, which don't require more than you already have at home.

TOE TRENDS

Toe-rrific guide is full of unique toenail designs from a French pedicure to sparkling glitter. We have created more than 150 styles for you, use any color of polish for any mood or occasion, a casual day to that special wedding day.

Best of all, you won't need any professional equipment or training. The days of uniform design and complicated applications are giving way to a fresh new trend – simple and dynamic. A regular nail polish brush that comes in any bottle and two or more nail polish colors of your choice will let you recreate any nail art idea from this book. You will be surprised how much you can do and how easy these beautiful designs are.

CREATIVE TOES

To help you to get started we have included some simple painting tips. In Toe-rrific guide we will show you how to think about setting the mood and picking up on the idea of where you are going or what you are celebrating.

This is just a small sampling of possibilities to the never-ending creations you can come up with. If you change your clothes, it will be easy to change your toes. A lot of our designs were inspired by our shoes, our clothes, nature and even things we had around the house. We are excited to see what you and other women come up with to express yourselves. Please use the card in the back of the book to share your new ideas or visit us on-line at www.toerrific.com.

We hope you have as much fun painting as we did making this book. And we hope your feet become a great asset to the rest of your body.

Elena & Cathleen

tools of the toes

The pages in front of you demonstrate what tools you can use for a home pedicure. You can keep your nail care kit basic or add a few extra tools or products if you like. Most of these items can be easily found in drug stores or even grocery stores.

nail polish remover

Gentle Nail Polish Remover
Acetone-Free
Dissolvant Doux
sans acétone

100 ml - 3.4 fl.oz.

cuticle scissors

cotton balls

basin with warm water

cuticle sticks

cuticle nipper

nail clipper

sea salts

emery board

toe separators

3

foot file

foot scrub

smoothing/buffer file

foot balm

base & top coat nail polish

PROFESSIONAL FOOT THERAPY

TEA TREE OIL
FOOT REPAIR BALM
AUSTRALIAN FORMULA
Aloe Vera & Chamomile

PROFESSIONAL
DOUBLE
TWIST
Fast-Drying
Base & Top Coat

Toe-rrific

color nail polish

jewels

glitter

bonder for applying
glitter & gems

BONDE

.75 fl. oz. e 22 m

nail brush

steps to a perfect...

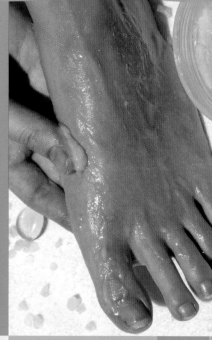

tip:

You can mix up a homemade scrub by combining 1/4 cup of oatmeal with 1/8 cup of water. Put on feet for 15 minutes for soft, smooth skin.

4

1

REMOVE OLD POLISH FROM NAILS

Begin by removing any old polish you may have on your toenails. Soak a cotton ball in polish remover and press the ball on the nail for a moment, then wipe away the nail polish in a circular motion. Try to find removers without acetone as they are more gentle on your nails.

3

EXFOLIATE

Once the water has softened the skin, exfoliate the bottoms of your feet with a pumice stone, or exfoliating scrub. Primary areas of concern are usually heels and balls of the feet where calluses can harden the skin. Be sure to clean the stone after each use and store it in a dry place.

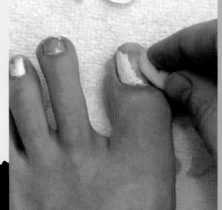

2

SOAK FEET

Fill a basin with a gallon of warm water. You can moisturize and soften the water with oils, or scented salts. As an alternative you can also use a tablespoon of baking soda and a teaspoon of bath oil. Remember that soapy water can be drying. Soak feet for 10-20 minutes. Pat feet dry with a towel.

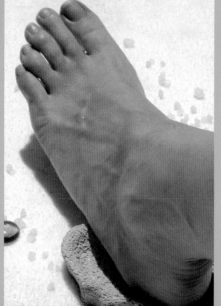

4

SCRUB

Use a gentle scrub applying it with your hands or a soft brush. Be careful not to scrub away too much of the outer layer of the skin that protects your feet. See the oatmeal recipe tip on the side for a homemade option to scrubbing your toes.

pedicure

5 MOISTURIZE

For deep moisturizing, apply a cream formula on your feet. When used after the soak, a lotion or cream application is absorbed quickly and helps minimize the return of rough hard skin. Repairing feet will be even more effective if after applying moisturizer you slip a pair of cotton socks over your feet and leave them on for 10-15 minutes.

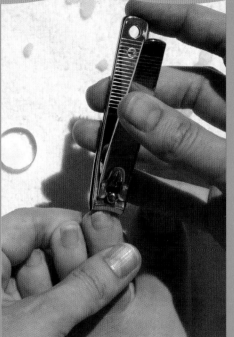

7 SHAPE NAILS

Using a nail file, shape your nails. Only file in one direction, since sawing back and forth will weaken the nails and cause them to split. Some nail files also have buffers on the other side. By gently buffing the nail, you stimulate circulation of blood to the surface, which gives it a healthy look. Buffing also helps to smooth ridges on your nails.

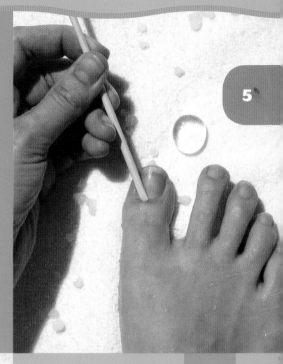

5

6 CUT TOENAILS

It's much easier to cut toenails after moisturizing. Length is a personal preference, but make sure the nail is shorter than the toe. Cutting toenails too short can lead to infections and ingrown nails. The last can be avoided by cutting toenails straight across.

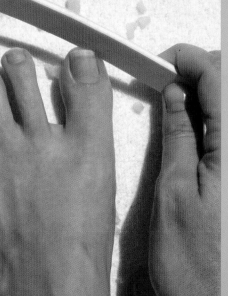

8 PUSH CUTICLES BACK

Using an orangewood stick push the cuticles back gently. Performing this step will be easier if you apply cuticle oil or any other body oil first. Pushing cuticles back visually extends the nail and gives it nice shape.

6

REMOVE OILS

9

Soak a cotton ball in a gentle polish remover, go over your toenails and then wipe off any residue with a dry towel. Remover will clean nailbeds from oily moisturizers and lotions, which would otherwise prevent nail polish from covering nails evenly.

CLEAR COAT

11

Always start by applying a clear base coat. It is generally used to fortify and protect the nail itself. A base coat prevents colored nail polishes from staining the nails and discoloring them, especially if you wear dark colors. Clear base coat creates a smooth surface for color. It also makes removing dark colors easier.

SEPARATE

10

Separate your toes using toe spacers or cotton balls. Tissue paper can also be woven in and out of the toes to separate them when preparing for polish application. There is a variety of toe spacers you can choose from. Find the one that is soft and works best for the size of your toes.

APPLYING

12

Apply first coat of colored polish. Remember to test the polish on paper to see how opaque it will appear. If it is too light but you want full coverage, you might need to put down a coat of white polish first. Let dry a minute or two. Remember to use plenty of polish to get a smooth finish.

SECOND COAT

13

Apply a second coat of polish if needed. Look for enamel paints that say "one coat" if you don't like to wait for the second coat to dry. Putting on a second coat will help nail polish last longer and will prevent it from chipping. Make sure to let toenails dry well between coats.

TOP COAT

15

Applying a clear top coat helps to protect the colored polish from chipping. If you have added any gems to your designs, transparent top coat will secure their position and prevent them from coming off. You can reapply top coat in a few days to keep designs looking fresh longer.

7

DESIGNS

14

Pick the design you want on your nails. Most start with a coat of one color and build onto the design. See pages 8-11 on painting steps and building up layers for fun designs. On the photo above simple polka dot pattern is easily created by adding white dots over the red polish base.

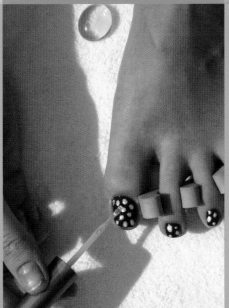

LET THOSE TOES DRY

16

Put your feet up and relax for a while to let your polish dry. A half hour is usually enough time though some polishes might take up to 24 hours to fully set. Make sure to read "Poor Soles" chapter on page 46 for maintaining those great looking feet now that you have mastered doing your own pedicure.

painting 101

test on paper

First try painting on paper to get a feeling for the brush. Don't get discouraged, you'll catch on fast. Check out some practice sketches below.

basic dot

Holding the brush upright to the nail, drop a little bit of polish onto the nail. For smaller dots use side corner of a brush.

basic stripe

Hold brush horizontally to the nail and draw a stripe across it. To create a perfect stripe you might need to draw on the skin around the nail. You can easily clean it off later with a cotton swab.

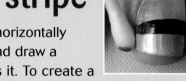

basic wave

Simple curves with enough polish on the brush can make any wave small or large. Again, practice a few times on paper to get the feel.

basic french

One of two ways is to paint one steady stroke across the top of the nail with a loaded brush (below). Second way is to draw a strip by filling in little segments. Above you can see that the stroke is made up of segments painted perpendicular to the nail.

basic square

Start with one stroke. Place your brush at a 90° angle and finish your corner by drawing second stroke from the edge of the first one.

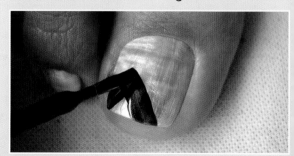

basic circle

A circle can be formed by drawing a half circle with one stroke and then another half

circle with the second stroke. If they don't line up perfectly, just circle around again or fix imperfections with the background color.

toothpick

A toothpick makes a great tool for those little touches you might need.

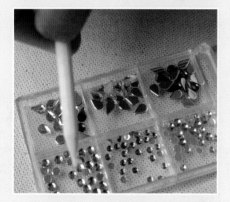

applying gems

Gems are an ideal solution if you want to add extra dimension and sparkle to the designs. Application steps are simple and take only a few minutes. After the polish is dry, apply a small dot of bonder on nail where the gem is to be placed. Pick up jewel with end of the damp orangewood stick and place it on bonder. You can dip end of application stick in water and then slightly wipe it off but honestly, saliva works better. Hold stone in place for a few seconds until dry. Once desired design is complete, apply topcoat and allow to dry.

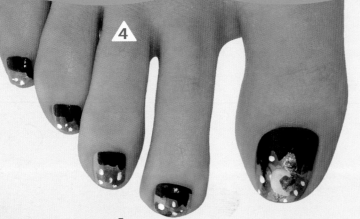

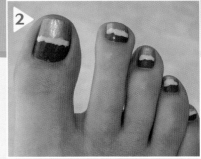
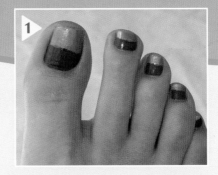

fruit punch

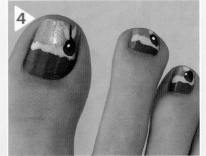
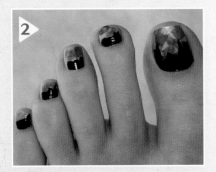

1 Paint half the nail orange and half blue. **2** Put yellow stripe in the middle of design. **3** Put a cherry dot and garnish it with a few green leaf brush strokes.

4 Add a stem to the leafs with black or any dark color. Put a white highlight on the cherry.
5 When polish is dry, apply bonder on yellow stripe. Sprinkle clear glitter above it to create an effect of a sugar rimmed glass.

starry night

1 Paint light blue then swirl dark blue on top. **2** Paint black landscape. **3** Paint the white moon first. The trick to a perfect moon is painting a large white dot and then placing smaller blue dot inside. Scatter stars around the moon. **4** Paint yellow over the white moon.

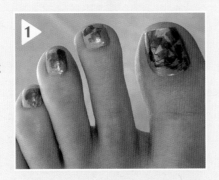
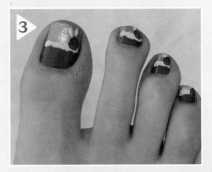

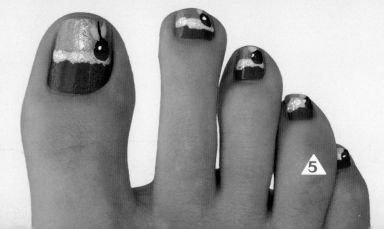

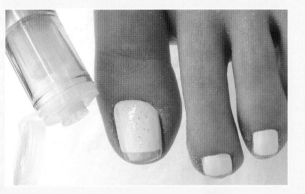

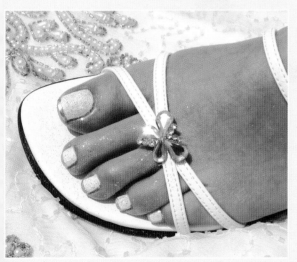

applying glitter

Applying loose glitter can be just what your toes need for some pizazz. There are special nail polishes that already contain glitter in them and they are used throughout the book. In comparison, loose glitter appears to have more shine because it's not covered with polish.

To use glitter on the nails let the polish dry thoroughly. Then put a bonder or any topcoat to the desired area of coverage. The glitter is applied with the fingertip, which gives better control than sprinkling. Surprisingly, with this technique, glitter holds on the nails for quite long. See below how the glitter still shines after five days.

❁ Loose glitter usually doesn't need a top coat of clear polish. The glitter will shine better and still stays on for days.

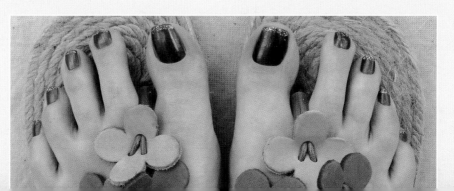

tip: If you get too much loose glitter on your feet simply wipe it off with a tissue. For those stubborn pieces, use a lint roller over your skin. The extra glitter around the nails can also be picked up with a lint roller. Just make sure that polish is dry.

ready for a new twist

On the following pages you'll find a wide variety of toenail designs.
Have fun experimenting with them and try your own ideas, too.

ON EACH PHOTO YOU WILL FIND A FLOWER ICON. IT SHOWS HOW SIMPLE OR COMPLEX A DESIGN IS TO CREATE. ONE PETAL DESIGNS ARE FAST AND 4 PETAL DESIGNS WILL TAKE SOME TIME.

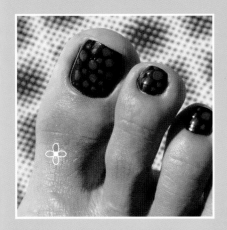

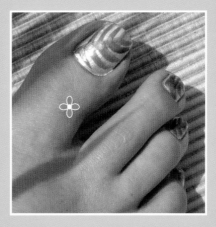

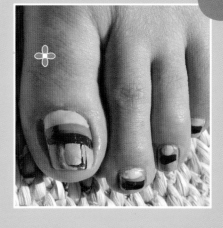

simple designs like polka dots require no drawing skills	simple designs like lines require basic drawing skills	a little more drawing involved	a little more difficult using shapes and angles
2 min	5 min	10 min	15 min

(Drying time is not included in above time estimates. Please follow the instruction on the nail polish bottle.)

yellows & oranges

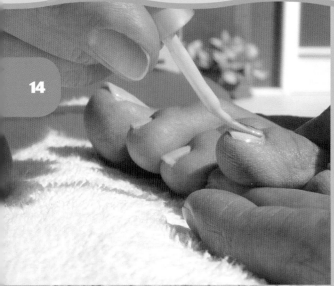

PAINTING YELLOWS AND ORANGES:
Yellows and oranges are pretty light colors and usually need a few coats to get a better coverage. Try applying white undercoat first to make the colors pop.

YELLOW FRENCH: Orange can make a fun look. Here a yellow French pedicure is jazzed up with some clear glitter thrown in while the polish was still wet.

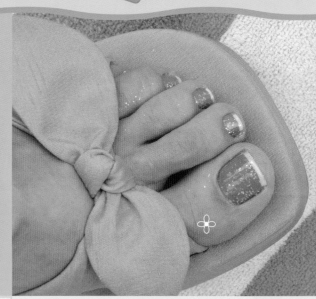

BLENDING POLISHES TOGETHER: Use two polishes and pour a little bit of each color out on a sheet of paper. Use a toothpick and mix together the polishes forming a range of various shades. Try blending other colors close in tone to see what neat combinations you can create.

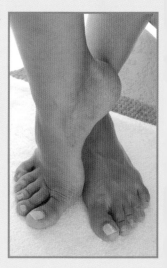

PUT SOME SUNSHINE ON YOUR TOES.
FOR FLARE USE BRIGHT AND HAPPY COLORS.

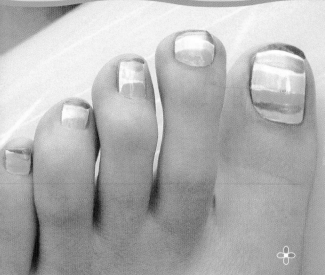

STRIPES AND PLAIDS: See page 8 for tips on painting straight lines. Don't be afraid to go over the skin and then wipe off the excess polish. Have fun using different colors in every combination you can imagine. When doing the plaid designs, transparent polishes work better as they overlay smoother.

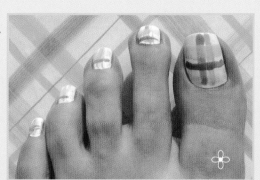

GEOMETRIC SHAPES: Making a combination of shapes is a fun way to pick up on different shoe designs and a variety of colors in your clothes. See pages 8 and 9 on painting techniques for making angles and curves in different shapes and designs.

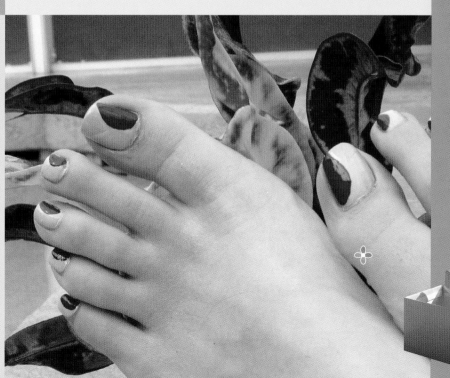

tip:

15

Going out to pick up a new pair of shoes? You might want to wait until afternoon as your foot swells when you walk and stand around during the day. Take time to try on both shoes. Feet can sometimes be different sizes and you need to shop for the larger one. Take the shoes for a walk around the store to see if they are comfortable.

tip: Citrus cuts through the hard soles of the feet and rubbing on a lemon or orange softens the skin. Soak your feet in a bath with a few tablespoons of lemon juice. It will help those tough feet turn baby smooth after a few times.

WATERMELON: Family picnics would make a great place to show off this design. Start with the green rim and add the inside red slice. Small strokes in a dark color make great seeds.

LEMONS: Squeeze this design in for a new look. Use a contrasting background color to make sure that the yellow will stand out.

CHERRIES: This design is a little harder, but worth the time. Paint the entire nail yellow, then add two red cherry dots. Add a couple of green leaves. Use a green dark enough to show up nicely on yellow. Finish by adding white highlights to the cherries.

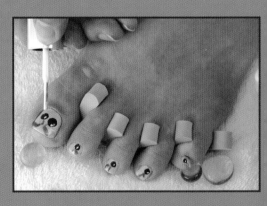

WHITE HIGHLIGHT TIP: Use a touch of white on any of fruity designs for a juicy highlight. What dimension you get!

JUST LIKE FRUIT SALAD, MIXING FRUITS AND FEET MAKES A TASTY TREAT.

LITTLE GREEN APPLES: Slice up a few pieces by painting a neutral background. Do a half circle of green with a lighter green inside. Add a few dark dots for seeds. It's apple pie!

PINEAPPLE: The symbol of welcome is a fun way to say "hi" to anyone. This design looks hard, but just think shapes and add lines with a toothpick for criss-cross.

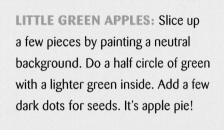

Try some other fruits we haven't. Lime, kiwi, bananas, plums, and many more.

Whatever you do, have fun expressing yourself.

GRAPES: Going to a wine tasting? This perfect design is just a group of dots with a few strokes of green at the top for leaves. Add white highlights and you have a whole bunch.

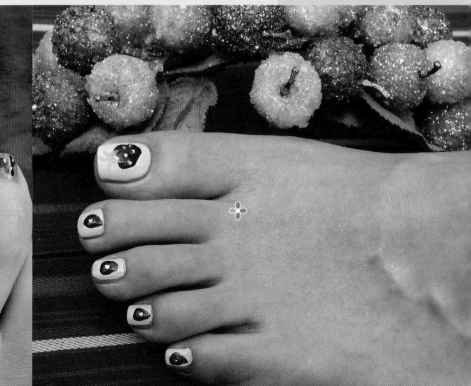

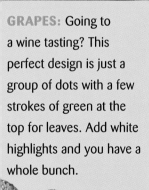

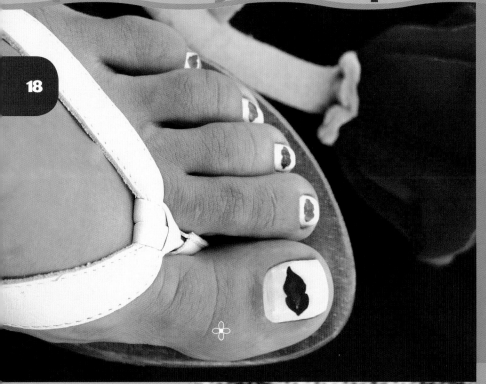

THE KISS: Who wouldn't want to kiss your lips? Paint a light background and then carefully angle the brush from the outside in to make some great lip shapes. Add pink to the inside to give a little dimension and separate the lips. Maybe add a tongue?

STRAWBERRY CHEESECAKE: Dripping with excitement, this design is really juicy. The two colors of pink give dimension, as well as the white highlight.

THE DOTS: This dark background makes the bright pink dots stand out. Pick a paint that is opaque enough to go over a dark color. The results can be stunning and you'll get hooked on dark colors.

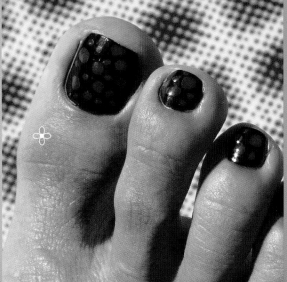

THE COTTON BALLS: This layered design will look nice with any color combination. Paint the entire nail one color and start to add the bands of color on top of one another. Try to pick opaque colors for the best results.

THE CROSSES: It is always fun to pick up on your shoes, even when they aren't sandals. You'll have fun in the locker room with this one. Simple crosses over multi-colors of pink are really fun.

THE NECKLACE: Make an elegant statement by picking up on your jewelry. These beads are easy to make with a series of dots. The top is accented with a French line in glitter to make the toes shine even more. Remember if there is also a buckle, button, bow or a gem on your shoe, it might be a nice idea for the toenail design.

tip: Put cotton balls between your toes if you don't have toe separators when painting your nails. Tissue paper can also work if woven in and out of the toes. See the list of resources on page 48 for more ideas.

FLOWERS: On the left there's a couple variations of pink flowers. The top has a gem in the center and the bottom one, a splash of yellow for a bright accent on any toe.

sweet tooth

PEPPERMINT CANDIES: These minty designs are just what you need for dull toes. Dressed up or down this is a good way to try something other than plain red.

CANDY-COATED: Wouldn't this look be beautiful with a pastel gown? Apply a solid yellow base coat followed by delicate colored ovals of various sizes. For light colors to show up paint ovals white first.

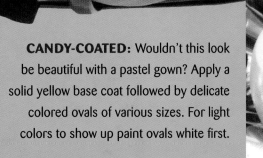

MAKE YOUR FEET LOOK SCRUMPTIOUS WITH CANDY-COATING FOR YOUR TOES.

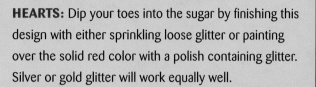

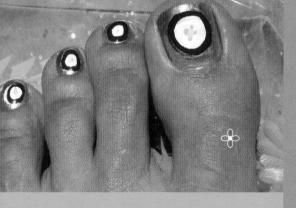

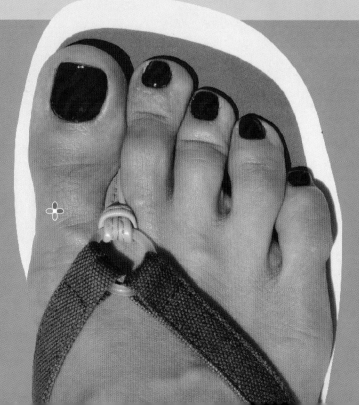

HEARTS: Dip your toes into the sugar by finishing this design with either sprinkling loose glitter or painting over the solid red color with a polish containing glitter. Silver or gold glitter will work equally well.

LICORICE: Two shades of red twisted together is a key to this design. Make one line, then follow that path with the other lines. What a fun look for your toes.

GUMMY BEARS: This bear is simple to create if you think about it as a combination of dots and ovals. Add highlight and shadows for dimension.

BON BONS: This wrapper can be a fun design to wrap your toes in. Use a toothpick to add some details of the paper wrapper and highlight the shape.

HARD CANDY FLOWERS: This hard candy design is not hard. Start with a solid pink nail, then a red circle and then a white circle on top of that. Add a few dots of green and yellow to make a flower design in the middle.

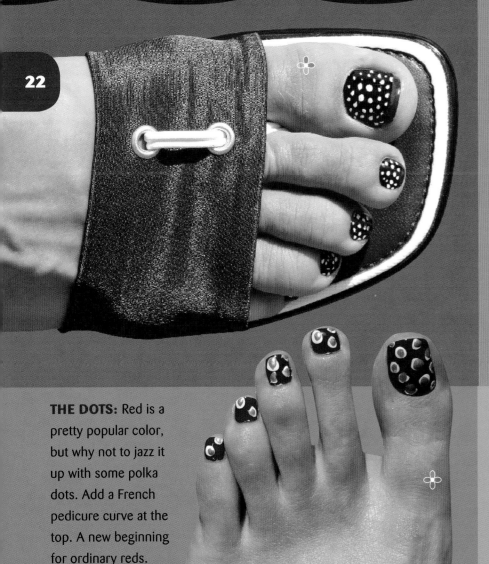

PETAL POWER: These petal empowered designs will make you feel like walking in a summer field all year round. Our flowers bloom in equal beauty whether in red or in a light color on red background. Flower designs can be easily created with a few dots or for bolder look with longer strokes. Add a gem in the center for extra pop.

THE DOTS: Red is a pretty popular color, but why not to jazz it up with some polka dots. Add a French pedicure curve at the top. A new beginning for ordinary reds.

RED TIP: Dip a Q-tip in remover and use to erase any unwanted polish. Red is a color that easily stains your skin. Make sure to use clear base coat to protect the nail.

1. STITCHES IN RED AND GOLD 2. TRIANGLE IN SHOE 3. SUNBURST GLITTER 4. STRAPS

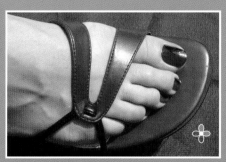

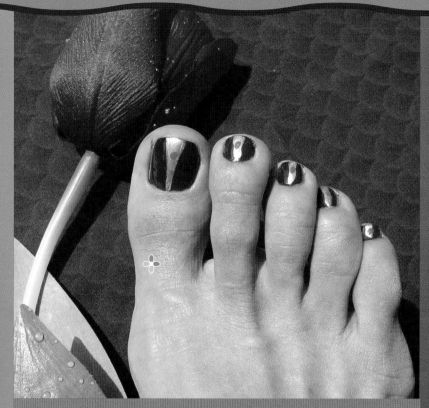

tip:

Any kind of foot rub feels great. Find out about reflexology in the library. This ancient art can point out different energy zones in your feet. Have fun.

THE COMPLETE ILLUSTRATED GUIDE TO REFLEXOLOGY

TULIP: This simple design can be done by either painting the nail a solid dark color and adding a light curved band in the middle, or painting the two sides over a lighter polish. A dot in the middle can be replaced by a gem or bead.

MATCHING YOUR SHOES: Let your shoes be your inspiration. Here details of the shoes like stitching or contrasting straps are accentuated by the toenail designs. Pick up on the shapes of your sandals and see what you can do. Reds are always exciting and excite emotions. Go for it!

beachy keen ☀

tip: Apply suntan oil over fresh polish. It will help the polish dry and protect it from smudging. Walking on a sandy beach barefoot is a great way to exfoliate and massage your feet.

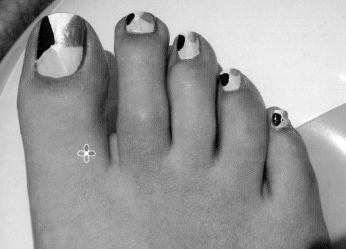

BEACH BALL: What a way to hit the beach. Go bouncing down the beach with this multi-color design. Minimize on colors or even go black and white if you want a classier look.

CATCH THE WAVE: This wave is a fun design for kicking back and relaxing. Use of purple, green and blue colors gives the nails a true tropical spa look.

H²O: This first water design was inspired by sky, water and sand. How simple but how cool. For extra chic, apply clear gold glitter nail polish above the sand stripe.

The second design is a little harder but worth the efforts. It will make you feel like surfing even on a calm day.

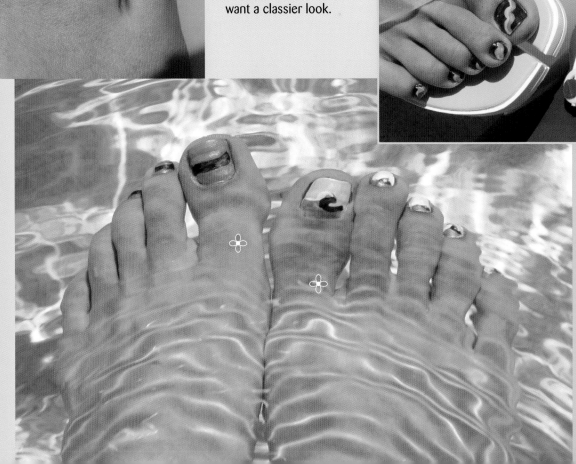

1. MANGO DAIQUIRI ANYONE? 2. PALM TREES SWAYING IN THE BREEZE 3. STARFISH ON CORAL

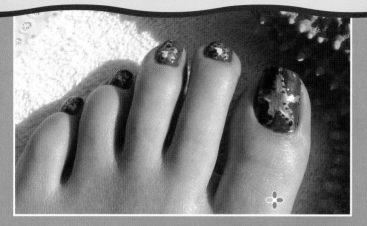

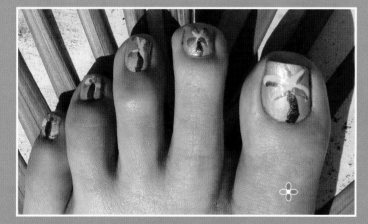

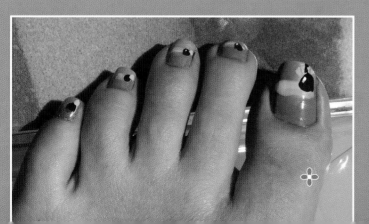

25

BIKINI: Everyone should wear a bikini. Why not? This red polka dot cutie is a two piece wonder made by painting the toes flesh color and adding red shapes dotted with white.

SAILBOAT: This simple curve is easy and quick to create when you are ready to have fun on the water.

TROPICAL TREASURES: Pick up on your surroundings and you'll fit right in. See fruit punch steps on page 10 for more details on painting.

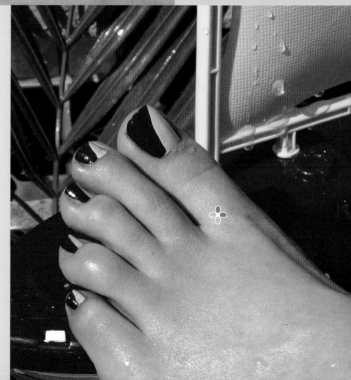

blue by you

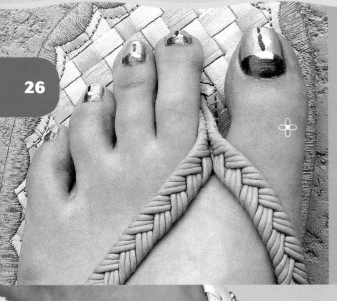

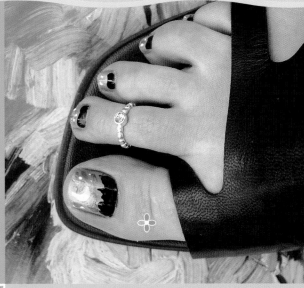

SAIL AWAY: Paint light blue at the top and dark blue at the bottom. This boat is just a few simple shapes with a dark line up the middle. Bon voyage.

BLUE JEAN BABY QUEEN: Just like your shoes, learn to pick up on your clothes design – and what's more popular than your jeans. Light or dark, new or worn, every pair of jeans in your closet can be an inspiration for your toes. Buckles, studs, patches, zippers, embroidery... go for it.

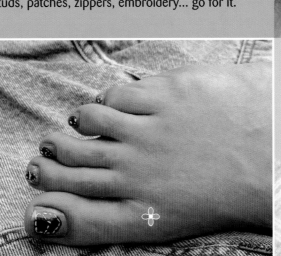

STARRY STARRY NIGHT: See for yourself that your toenails can be as beautiful as a work of art. Check out painting steps on page 10 to see this design in more detail.

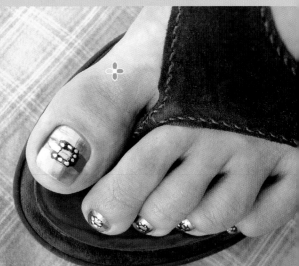

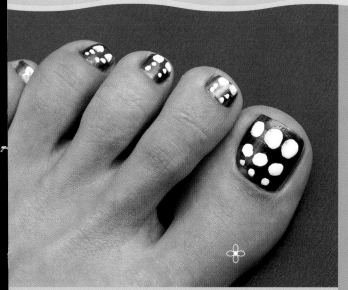

FLORAL DESIGN: Pattern of flowers in this nail design is soft and feminine. Let your fantasy rule and create your dream toe gardens in blue.

STRIPES OF GLITTER: Blues can be elegant too. This subtle design looks great with silver and gold.

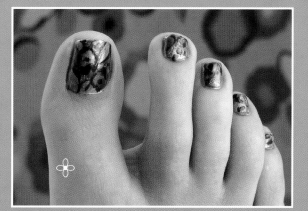

MULTI-SHAPED DOTS: This stylish design just takes a little good judgement to draw. The key of this "art deco inspired" design is in it's simplicity which makes it a fit even for a business suit.

GEOMETRICAL DESIGN: A pink gem or a pink nail polish dot will add playfulness to the strict shapes of the design. Keep in mind that vertical and oblique lines make your nails look longer.

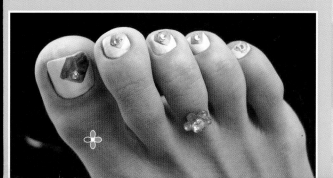

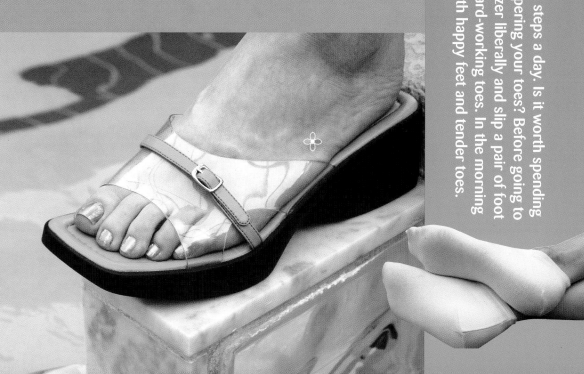

You take over 8000 steps a day. Is it worth spending a little time on pampering your toes? Before going to bed, apply moisturizer liberally and slip a pair of foot socks over those hard-working toes. In the morning you will wake up with happy feet and tender toes.

all natural

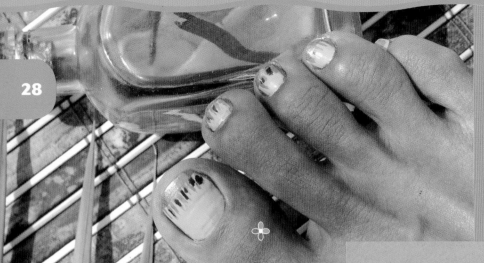

GREENS: These designs use a hard color to paint. Too much green can look too fungusy. Keep the design in mind and add other colors to accent the green.

GRASS: This natural design is easy to make with wisps of green strokes coming down vertically on the toe. Gold curve on the top sparkles like sunny day.

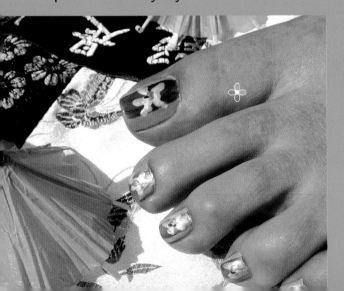

BERRIES: Paint two colors of green with a natural curve. Add berries to the sides. Experiment with different colors for berries.

FLOWER: A little feel of the orient is reflected in this design. The white delicate petals of the flower stand out against green stripe. Lighter color on the sides of the nail softens the look.

1. PALM LEAF ON WHITE BACKGROUND 2. SEA SALT COLORS 3. LEAFY INSPIRATION

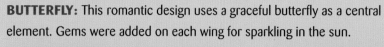

BUTTERFLY: This romantic design uses a graceful butterfly as a central element. Gems were added on each wing for sparkling in the sun.

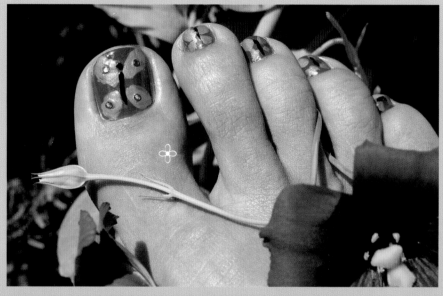

TURTLE: How cool is this turtle design? Paint your nails solid purple and put a green circle in the middle. Make arms, legs and head with dots. Light blue was painted over the shell for dimension.

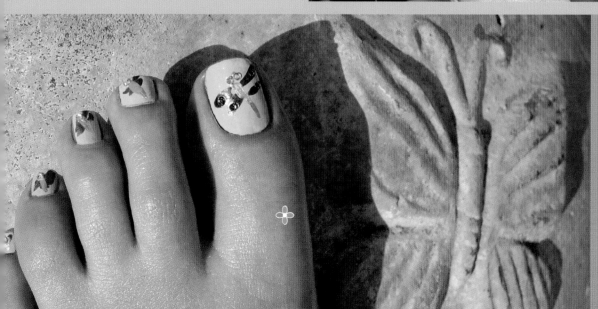

DRAGONFLY: Nature provides us with great inspiration. This dragonfly has purple wings crowned with gems. Smaller stones are used for the eyes. Silver chrome makes a great color for the body of dragonfly and easily goes over any nail polish.

tip:

29

Olive oil makes a great moisturizer and can be used just like regular skin lotion. It contains antioxidants, vitamins and has regenerating power. Olive oil softens and tones the skin. It is also believed to be a proven sunburn remedy.

purple passion

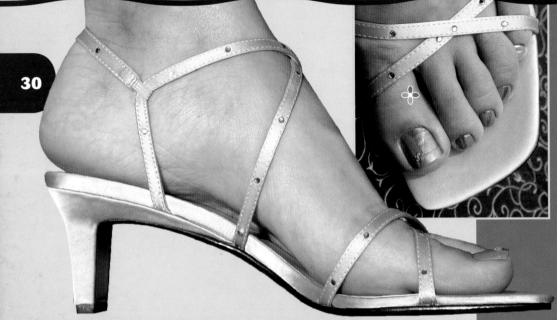

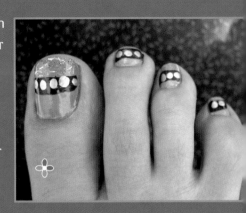

SHOOTING STAR: The shoe design was the inspiration for this purple persuasion. It's very simple and combines two nail polish colors with a star shaped gem on top.

DOTS: This fun design will work with any color combination. Paint the toes purple and add a band of a darker color. Silver dots go over the band while silver glitter polish decorates the top of the nail.

TROPICAL: Just perfect for that luau. Paint the nail a solid color and then combine stripes, waves, dots and dashes to make this fun design work for you. Pick colors that easily go over one another.

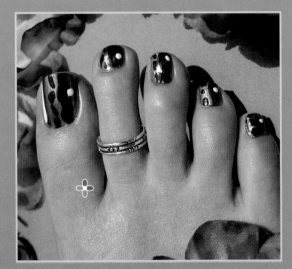

SWIRLS: This modern design is too hip. Paint the nail a solid chrome silver, then add the swirls of pink and purple over it. Groovy Baby!

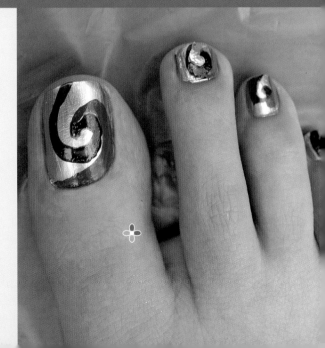

BEADS: This dimensional design is so easy. Pick a neutral color for the background and pick contrasting colors for the dots on top. Build up a few layers of dots for each color. The more random the better.

ORIENTAL EXPRESS: This quick design is just what you need when wearing some of the latest Eastern fashions. Paint the nail a solid dark color and let the brush strokes flow freely from thick to thin lines to create the Asian feel.

31

It's a good idea, when you buy a new pair of shoes, to rub the hard soled bottoms with sandpaper. Do this after you've definitely decided you don't need to take them back! Sandpaper will make surface less slippery and will add confidence to your walk.

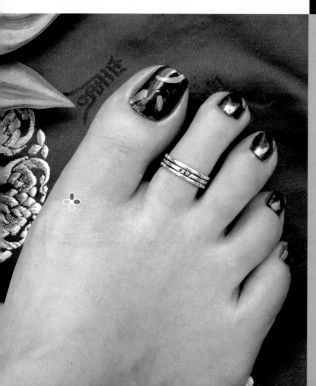

SUNSET: This design picks up the colors of a sunset. How perfect for a walk on the beach. Paint the whole nail pink and add the stripes of color and the sun.

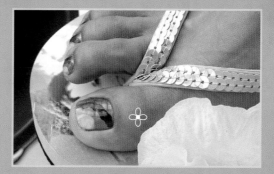

GO GRAPE: Why not do a French manicure in purple and pink? What a fun design. Use the side of the toothpick to create the pin stripes across the nail.

tip:

Seal the gems you put on with a top coat which helps them last longer. Allow enough time to dry before putting your shoes on as the gems can easily get bumped out of place.

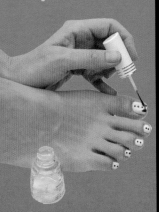

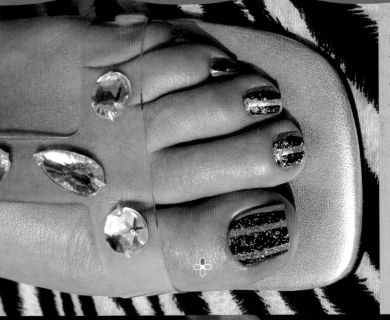

MUSIC WAVES: This fun wavy design adds extra dimension to the nails and is perfect for disco night. Brighten in up with gems or polish dots.

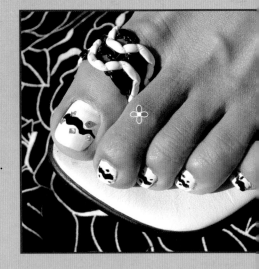

ON THE PROWL: When you're in the limelight on the dance floor, these toes will really glitter. Paint white with black stripes, and then put a silver glitter polish coat over the entire nail.

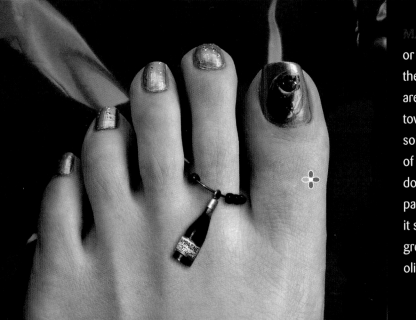

MARTINI: Shaken or stirred? Whatever the drink, these toes are ready to hit the town. First paint the solid green oval on top of pink base coat. Put down a white dot and paint over it with red so it stays bright. A light green highlight brings olive alive.

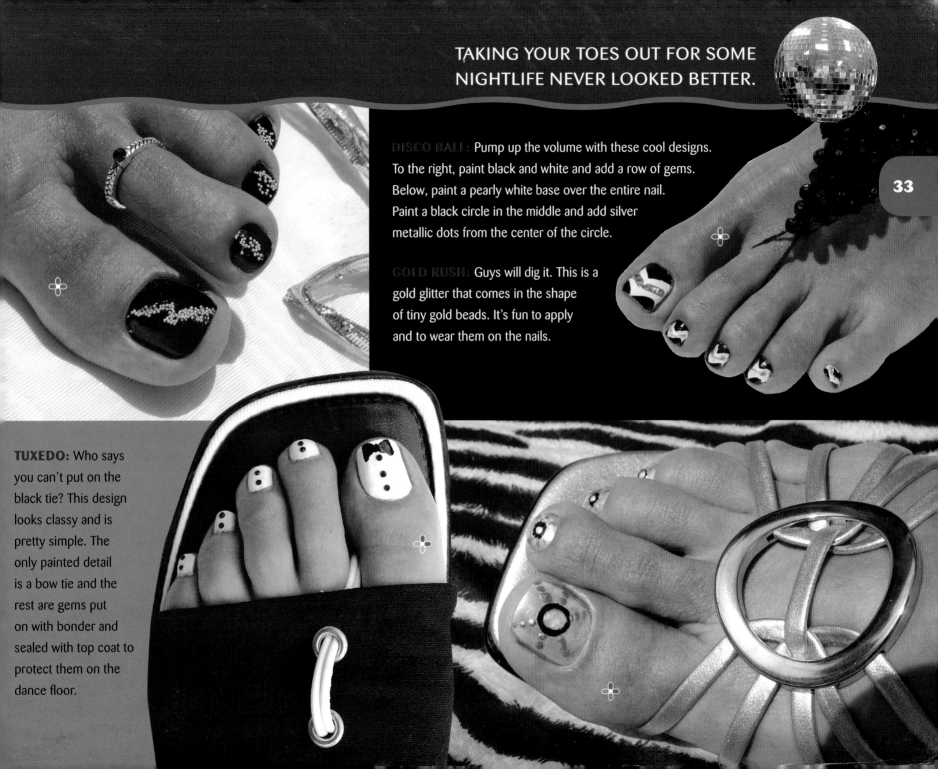

TAKING YOUR TOES OUT FOR SOME NIGHTLIFE NEVER LOOKED BETTER.

33

DISCO BALL: Pump up the volume with these cool designs. To the right, paint black and white and add a row of gems. Below, paint a pearly white base over the entire nail. Paint a black circle in the middle and add silver metallic dots from the center of the circle.

GOLD RUSH: Guys will dig it. This is a gold glitter that comes in the shape of tiny gold beads. It's fun to apply and to wear them on the nails.

TUXEDO: Who says you can't put on the black tie? This design looks classy and is pretty simple. The only painted detail is a bow tie and the rest are gems put on with bonder and sealed with top coat to protect them on the dance floor.

chocolate

CHOCOLATE COVERED CHERRY: This is a perfect design to try with your brown and cherry colored polishes. Paint the toes light brown. Then add the cherry circle and the dark brown swash for the outside. White highlights will give it that glossy feeling.

CHOCOLATE DRIZZLES: Here's an idea for having fun with chocolate toppings. Frost your toes with a brown or white chocolate and drizzle it with a toothpick.

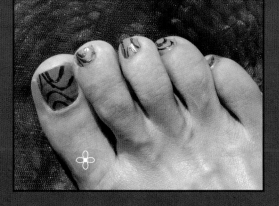

M&M's®: These won't melt in your hands but on your toes. This simple design is fun. Paint entire nail dark chocolate, then add dots in white. Use bright colors over the white to make your toe M&M's® look just like real.

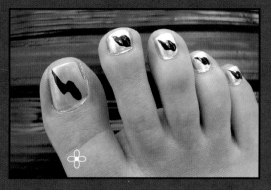

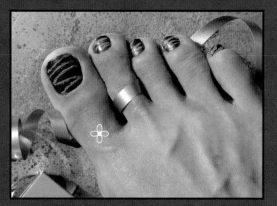

1. LIGHT CHOCOLATE SWIRL 2. CHOCOLATE FROSTING 3. DARK CHOCOLATE SWIRL

35

BOX OF CHOCOLATES: You'll never know what you'll get when you try this perfect confection. Paint the nail dark chocolate and add the lighter chocolate swirl on top. Try combinations of various colors from milk chocolate to white with darker or lighter swirls.

GOLD WRAPPER: The chocolate candy wrapper was the inspiration for this nail design. Paint the nail gold and put the dark chocolate over the gold. See the painting tips on pages 8 for angle tricks.

tip: When space is tight and your brush is too thick, use a toothpick to create your whirls and swirls. Wooden toothpicks seem to soak up the paint and hold it better than the plastic ones. Experiment and have fun.

POUND CAKE: This is a great design for a tea party. Paint the nails with a cream base, then add the chocolate cake layers. Don't be afraid to go over the skin, as it's easy to wipe off polish with remover.

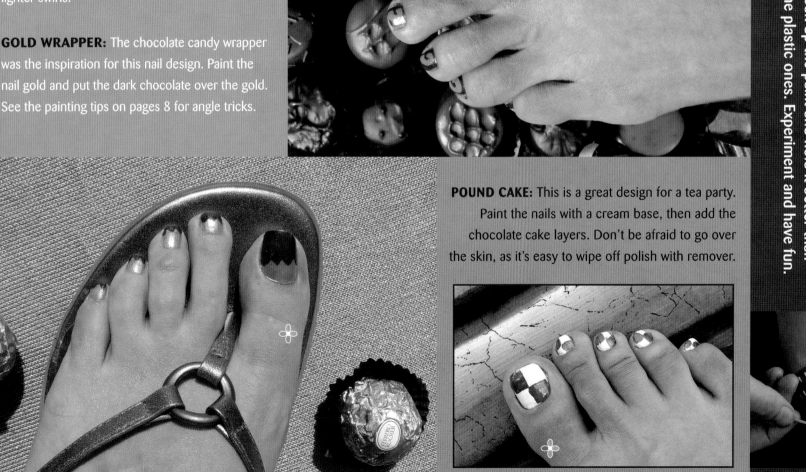

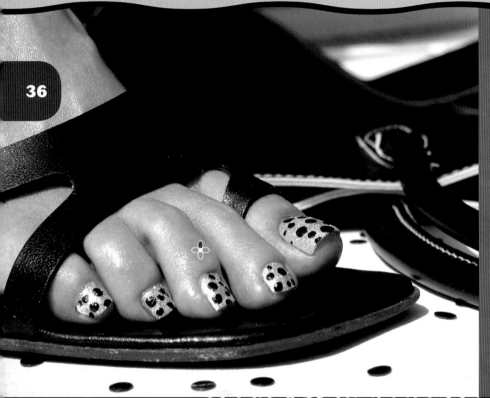

FLOWER PETALS: Start by applying a base coat of black nail polish. Don't forget about the protective coat of clear polish as black can easily stain the nails. Add white flower petals after the black has dried well. Top off the middle of the flowers with pink jewels or color dots of your choice.

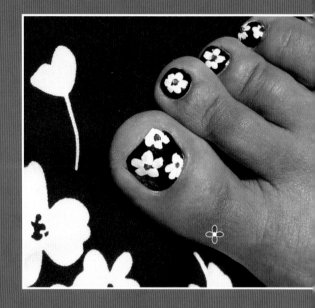

WHITE STRAP: This design picks up on the shoe strap. Paint white circles on black and dot in middle.

DOTS: Often associated with wealth and elegance, black dots can be dressed up or down. On the design above a white frosty base is dotted with solid black. For the shooting star add the swash and you are ready to show off.

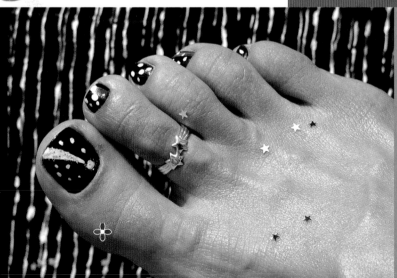

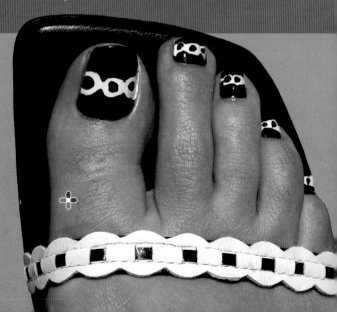

BLACK REALLY IS MAGIC.
SEE ALL THE POSITIVE AND NEGATIVE COMBINATIONS.

THE EYE: What a sexy looking design. This Egyptian eye is created with a few strokes of black polish on white background.

BUBBLES: This simple design is just really dots of different sizes with highlights. You can do it with other colors and create a fun effect.

DARK POLISHES:
If you can't find a black polish you need, other dark colors like dark brown, red or purple (see the design below) make a great substitute.

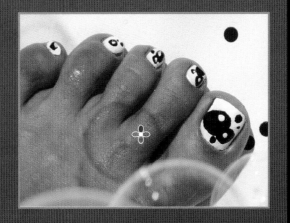

SCULPTURE:
Paint the entire toe black and then paint a white solid oval in the middle. Go back and paint the black stripes through the white oval.

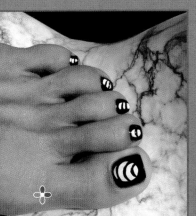

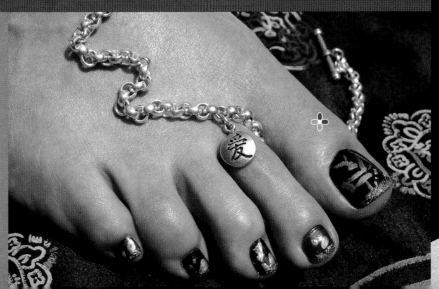

tip : Use white vinegar to whiten nails. Soak for 30 minutes as often as needed to brighten the surface. Lemon juice is another way for removing discolored areas. You can soak nails in water with lemon juice or gently rub nails with a slice of lemon.

wedding bells 🔔

tip: Use a warm milk bath for a royal foot soak. The natural oils in the milk will cleanse the feet and make them feel silkier. You can sprinkle in a few flower petals for aroma. What a luxurious tip for the bride to be.

THE RING: Why not tie the knot on your toes too? Paint the entire nail with an ivory bone china polish. Paint the big toe nail with a gold band across it and the tops of the other nails with gold. Place a dot of gold polish on the band and add a large gem in the center.

SILVER LINING: Your clouds will be full of silver linings if you try this easy design. Paint a white base coat and add a French tip in silver. When the polish is still tacky, sprinkle in a clear glitter for that shiny look.

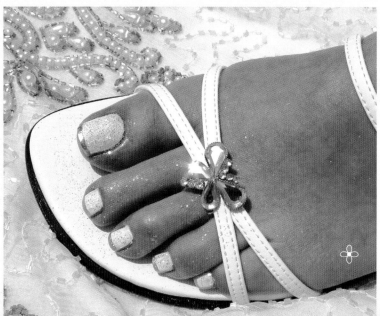

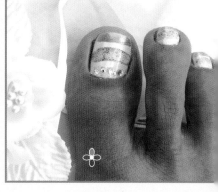

BEADED GOWN: Remember to pick up on the designs in your gown. A row of beads or pearls would look great on your toes, too.

WHAT A SPECIAL DAY. TREAT YOURSELF TO
SOMETHING SPECIAL ALL THE WAY DOWN TO YOUR TOES.

39

SOMETHING BLUE:
Here is a way to borrow
something blue. These
blue gems are placed on
top of gold lines .

WEDDING BELLS:
What an idea for ringing
in this special day. Paint
a gold bell and embellish
it with tiny gold beads.

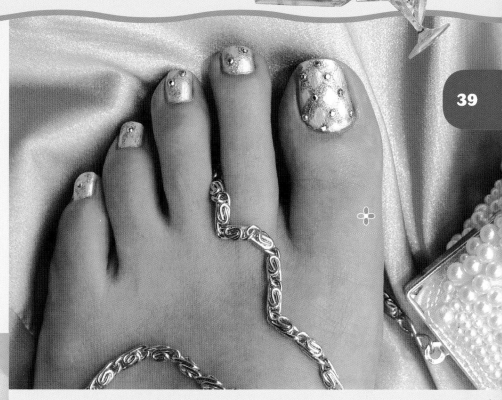

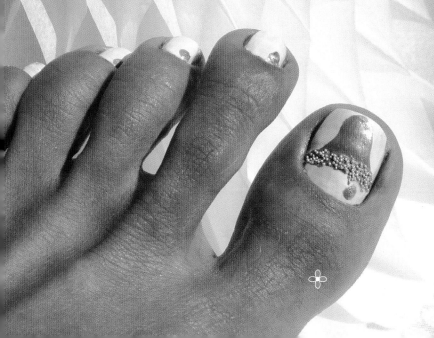

GOLD PATTERNS:
The design above is a beautiful
way to present your toes.
Paint frosty white polish over
nail. Make a gold lattice with
criss-cross stripes of gold glitter
polish. Place gold gems or
beads where the lines intersect.

TEA ROSE: Pick up on the design of a wedding pattern. How delicate.

twinkle toes

tip: Add a toe ring for extra twinkle. There are rings that come with the invisible stretch band, adjustable rings that wrap around the toe and sized toe rings. See the Resources in the back of the book for toe ring companies.

RHINESTONE RING: This row of gems was placed in a band after the toe was painted with solid gold. Gold glitter polish was applied underneath the band.

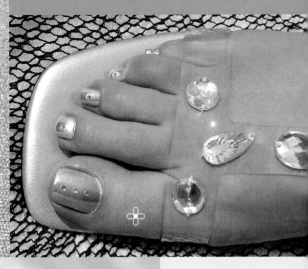

GLITTER HEART:

This heart was created by painting the nail a white color, then the pink glitter polish was applied to the negative space. What a romantic way to go to the prom or any occasion needing a little extra heart.

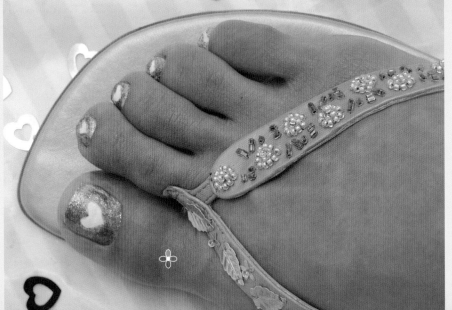

GLITTER BANDS:

The nails were painted with frosty white and then a silver band was added as a stripe down the middle of each nail. A few clear gems were placed on the silver stripe to give it an embossed look.

MOROCCAN INSPIRATION: Beautiful colors and gems make a passionate combination in this design. A French curve in purple glitter polish was painted above red base coat. The rows of red and purple gems were applied to set off the design. Picking a gem the same color as the nail polish always adds a delicate touch.

PINK GLITTER CIRCLES: This design was created with two shades of nail polishes and loose pink glitter. Try same shapes in different colors. To learn more about applying glitter, turn to the special section on page 11.

CROSSES: The buckle of the shoe clearly gave an idea for this design. White polish was painted as a base color. Then red and silver cross braces were added. Gems were placed within the cross to add extra dimension. Finally a clear coat was applied for protection.

41

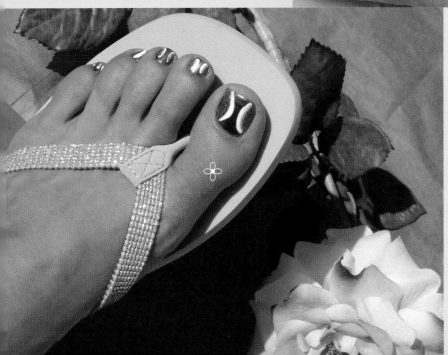

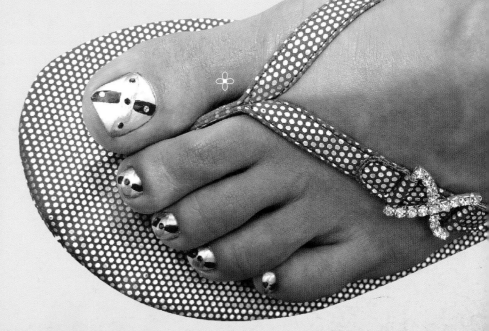

love notes... ♥

tip: Walking on the beach scrubs your feet naturally and is a good exercise for your calf muscles. The salt water is also a refreshing way to keep those toes cool.

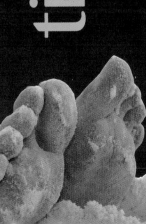

BROKEN HEART:
If you don't wear your heart on your sleeve, maybe on your toes. This girly design starts with a dark color base. Then two bright pink pieces of the heart are drawn above it. Add white highlights and shadows for dimension.

HE LOVES ME: He loves me not. Hopefully this works out just right. Paint a solid pink base and add petals around a middle. At the end add the orange center in a circle shape.

PS I LOVE YOU:
Initial your toes for that personal touch. Here an ivory base was painted and the initials were added in a dark color. Dark browns and blues are good ink colors to pick for this design.

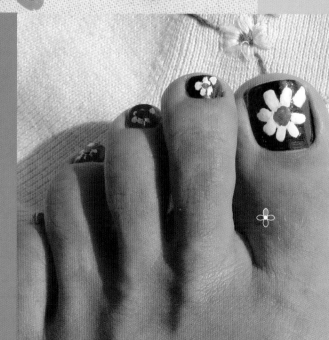

specialty toes

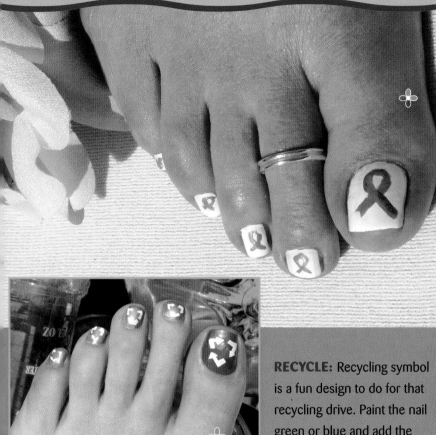

BREAST CANCER AWARENESS: What a nice way to show your support for the breast cancer awareness movement. Would be a good idea to wear to the Race for the Cure or other charity benefits. This design consists of a white background and a pink ribbon painted on top of it. Use red polish for highlights.
For more information about Breast Cancer Research Foundation go to www.bcrfcure.org

EARTH DAY: This design can be a first step in taking action to protect the earth. Apply a coat of light blue polish. If you don't have desired shade, mix dark blue and white polishes together. Paint the earth with a dark blue circle and add green dots for the continents.

RECYCLE: Recycling symbol is a fun design to do for that recycling drive. Paint the nail green or blue and add the white arrows.

GRADUATION: The perfect idea for the graduate ready to go out into the new world. This black tassel is decorated with gold glitter on the bottom edge to catch the eye.

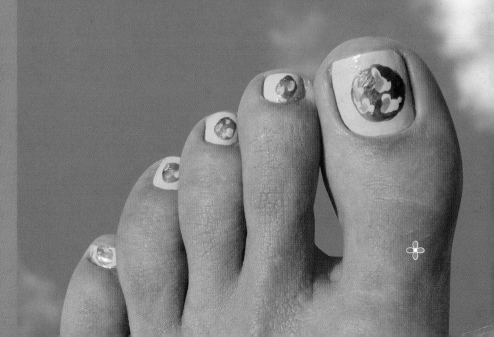

44

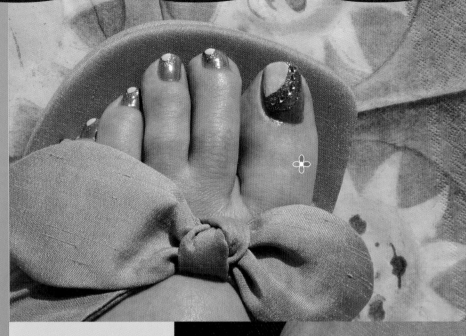

WAKE UP TIME: This bright sunny design will make anyone smile. Paint the entire nail solid orange. On the tip, paint a yellow half circle. If your yellow polish is not opaque, paint half circle with white first. The orange gems and some clear nail polish with glitter were added for dimension and shine. Oh sunny day.

EGG-CELLENT BREAKFAST: This early morning favorite is just a few easy steps away. Paint the nail with dark purple. The egg white can be made of large white dots. For the yolk, drop an orange dot in the center of the egg white, and then a yellow dot above it.

COFFEE BREAK: If you like coffee, you'll love this eye opener. Paint the entire nail a light beige color. Add brown coffee beans with two strokes of the brush. Who needs caffeine?

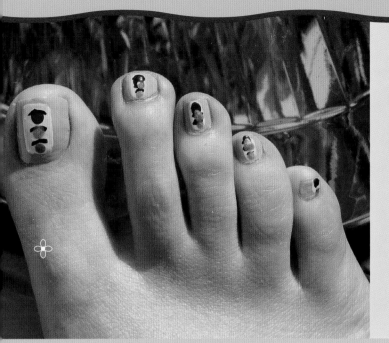

DRIVE TO WORK: This traffic light is a great way to make your drive to work more enjoyable. Paint the nails powder blue. Then add a yellow rectangle over the blue. See the painting spread on page 8 for angle tips. Finish it off by painting black arches and dots for lights.

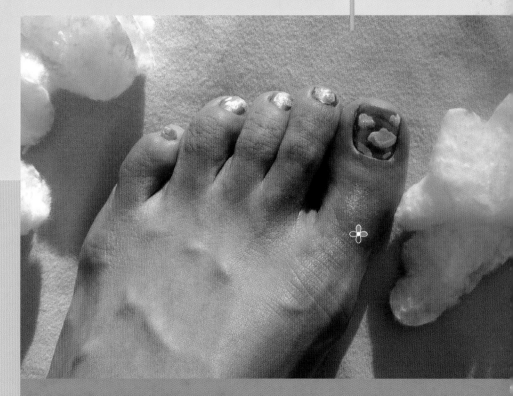

STOP AT THE MALL: Stop by the mall in this cute shopping bag design. What a bargain.

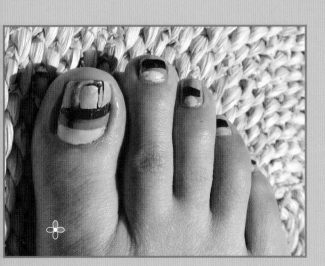

SWEET DREAMS: When you are ready to count some sheep, sit down and paint dreamy clouds on your toes. Apply light blue first, and then paint dark blue strokes for the shadows under the clouds. Add the white clouds slightly overlapping the dark blue shadows. Throw in some silver linings if you want.

poor soles...

tip:
A toothbrush with any nice hand or foot soap makes a great tool for getting into those hard to reach areas like under the nails or between the toes.

Here are some tips on maintaining your toe-rrific toes through out the day:

WHEN YOU WAKE UP: If you can't wear sandals during the day, pick cotton socks. Make sure that your shoes are made from non-synthetic materials. It is important for your feet to breathe. Putting some talcum powder in your shoes can help soak up extra moisture. Don't always wear the same shoes. Give them some time to air out from the day before.

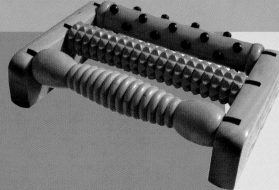

AT YOUR DESK: Keep a roller under your desk that can help give you a foot massage when you are getting tired. There are lots of great products for foot massage and foot care, see page 50 of the Resources section.

WASHING: After washing, always dry the feet thoroughly, especially in between your toes, where the build-up of moisture hides. If you are in a public place like a gym, wear flip-flops into the shower or near the pool to protect feet from bacteria.

EXERCISE: Don't forget how important exercise is for great looking feet. Doing the basic runner's stretch will increase flexibility in your feet (With one leg bent behind and the other straight in front lean over the front leg with the back straight). A few yoga classes during the week will be great for better blood circulation.

EPSOM SALTS: To relieve tension and puffiness in feet after a hard day of work soak them in a bath with Epsom salts. You can easily find these restorative salts at any drug store.

EAT RIGHT: Eating healthy adds to the glow of your skin. If you need strength in your nails, eating jello is a good source of gelatin.

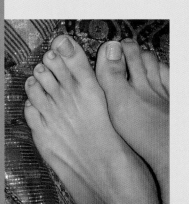

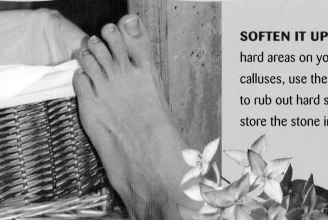

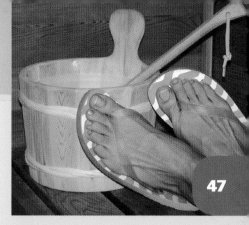

47

SOFTEN IT UP: If you develop hard areas on your feet like calluses, use the pumice stone to rub out hard spots. After use store the stone in a dry place.

PAY ATTENTION: Keep an eye on your feet. If you notice any changes, like new bumps, or feel pains consult with a doctor.

REFLEXOLOGY: If you want to get a therapeutic foot massage, try reflexology. Massage directs the flow of negative energy out through the toes by stimulating energy points on the feet. Learn more about reflexology at the library or online.

SLEEP: Get plenty of sleep. Before going to bed, apply foot lotion or petroleum jelly liberally and slip a pair of foot socks to soften and repair feet overnight.

foot reflexology
EUCALYPTUS & MINT
FOOT SOAK

PREVENT SMELLY FEET: Soak your feet in strong black tea for 30 minutes a few times a week. The tannic acid in the tea kills the bacteria and closes the pores, keeping your feet dry longer. Tea time...

resources

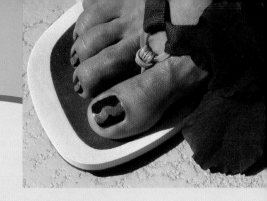

TOOLS OF THE TRADE

Diamancel Foot Callus Files
www.diamancel.com

**HoMedics Spa Foot Care &
Foot Massagers**
www.homedics.com

Lippmann Collection Nail Treatment
www.lippmanncollection.com

Sephora Nail Treatment Kit
www.sephora.com

Tweezerman Pedicure Tools
www.tweezerman.com

NAIL POLISH

Avon Nail Polishes
www.avon.com

Barielle Nail Polishes
www.barielle.com

Clinique Nail Polish
www.clinique.com

Creative Nail Design Nail Polish
www.creativenaildesign.com

Essie Nail Polish
www.essie.com

Estée Lauder Nail Polish
www.esteelauder.com

Hard Candy Nail Polish
www.hardcandy.com

Jane Nail Polish
www.janecosmetics.com

Lancôme Nail Polish
www.lancome.com

Lorac Nail Polish
www.loraccosmetics.com

L'oreal Nail Polish
www.lorealparis.com

M.A.C. Nail Polish
www.maccosmetics.com

Mary Kay Nail Polish
www.marykay.com

Maybelline Nail Polish
www.maybelline.com

Misa Nail Polish
www.misacosmetics.com

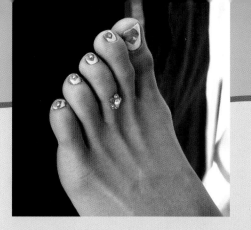

Nicole Nail Polish
www.nicole-by-opi.com

N.Y.C.
www.newyorkcolor.com

Orly Nail Polish
www.orlybeauty.com

OPI Nail Polish
www.opi.com

Pinkie Swear Nail Polish
www.pinkieswear.com

Poshe Top Coat
www.poshe.com

Revlon Nail Polish
www.revlon.com

Sally Hansen Nail Polish
www.sallyhansen.com

SpaCadet Nail Polish
www.spacadet.com

Ulta Nail Lacquer
www.ulta.com

Yves Rocher Nail Polish
www.yvesrocher.com

Zoya Nail Polish
www.artofbeauty.com/zoya

NAIL POLISH REMOVERS

Cutex Nail Polish Remover
www.cutexnails.com

Luca Nail Polish Remover Pads
www.myluca.com

Mavala Nail Polish Remover
www.mavala.com

The Stripper Nail Polish Remover
www.lippmanncollection.com

JEWELS, GEMS AND TOE RINGS

Dina's Nail Art Jewels
www.dinasnailart.com

Fing'rs Glue and Gems
www.fingrs.com

Italian Jewelry Toe Rings
www.snailsitalianjewelry.com

Powder Polish Nail Jewels
www.powderpolish.com

Girly Q Toe Rings
www.girlyq.com

Toe Brights Toe Ring Jewelry
www.toebrights.com

Toerings Fitted Toe Rings
www.toerings.com

FOOT CARE PRODUCTS

Ahava Dead Sea Cosmetics
Bath Salts & Foot Cream
www.ahava.com

Dr. Scholl's Products
Pedicure Creams, Scrubs & Lotions
www.drscholls.com

Earth Therapeutics, Ltd.
Moisturizing Foot Socks & Lotions
www.earththerapeutics.com

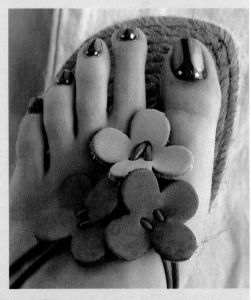

EO Essential Oil Products
Foot Scrub, Lotion, Balm & Spray
www.eoproducts.com

Essie Cosmetics , Ltd.
Cuticle Oil & Nail Treatments
www.essie.com

Estelina's Pedicure Products
www.estelinas.com

EzFlow Nail Systems
www.ezflow.com

Footherapy Foot Care Products
Foot Scrub, Powder, Soak & Lotion
www.queenhelene.com

Freeman Bare Foot Products
Foot Soaks, Scrubs & Lotions
www.freemancosmetics.com

Gena Salon Pedicure System
Soak Bathes, Lotions & Liquid Talc
www.qualityessentials.com

Göt2b Spa
Foot Soak, Gel, Scrub & Cream
www.got2bspa.com

Happy Roller for Feet
31055 Huntwood Avenue
Hayward, CA 94544

Kiss Products, Inc.
Pedicure Tools, Foot Scrub & Lotion
www.kissusa.com

Lucky Chick Pampering Products
Foot Soak, Mist, Scrub & Lotion
www.luckychick.com

pH Beauty Labs
Totally Nutty Foot Care
www.totallynutty.com

Philosophy Cosmetics
Pumice Foot Scrub &
Exfoliating Foot Cream
www.philosophy.com

Footherapy Foot Care Products
Foot Scrub, Powder,
Soak & Lotion
www.queenhelene.com

Zents Luxurious Spa Products
www.zents.com

SHOPPING GUIDE

If you want **MOISTURE** for your toes look for: almond oil, calendula oil, cocoa butter, coconut oil, honey, jojoba oil, milk, olive oil, primrose oil, and shea butter.

If you want products with **ANTIBACTERIAL** properties for your toes look for: aloe vera oil, apple-cider vinegar, arnica cream, chamomile, and grapefruit seed extract.

If you want **ANTI-INFLAMMATORY** products look for: arnica cream, camphor oil, Epsom salts, green tea, horse chestnut, and lemon juice.

If you want **DEODORIZING** for your toes look for: blue chamomile, magnolia buds, and rose petals.

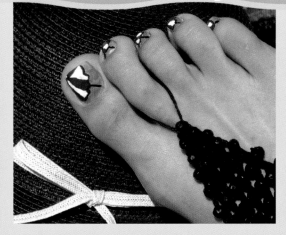

If you want products with **STIMULATING** properties for your toes look for: eucalyptus oil, ginger, and peppermint oil.

If you want to **REJUVENATE** your toes look for: papaya and tea tree oil.

If you want to **PREVENT SWEATY FEET**: wear cotton socks or natural-fiber socks, and check out advice on page 47.

SHOE BUYING GUIDE

Select a shoe by trying it on, not by the size marked on the shoe.

Buy shoes with firm arch support.

Shop for shoes later in the day. Your feet are at their smallest in the morning and will swell slightly as the day progresses.

Walk in the shoes for a while to make sure they are comfortable and won't cause blisters.

Try on both shoes. One foot might be a little larger than the other.

Buy shoes made of natural materials (i.e. leather, cotton or the like) as these materials breathe.

about us

Happy Women Publishing Company was started by Elena Prostova and Cathleen Shaw. Their mission has been to find great ways to make women look and feel beautiful.

Besides loving to paint toes, Cathleen Shaw, loves to design books. After graduating from the Columbus College of Art & Design, she went on to design hundreds of books for F&W Publishing, Prentice Hall, McGraw-Hill and Rockport. This is the first book in a series of many that are meant for women to show how beautiful they can be.

Cathleen now lives in Sarasota, Florida where she can show off her toes on the beach and enjoy her husband Steve and son Maxx.

Elena Prostova has graduated from Kazan State University where she was studying modern literature. After working in advertising and being Editor In Chief of the lifestyle magazine "Expressions" she found her true love in graphic design to which she stays true for more than five years. Recently she found out that toenails are the best canvas for creative ideas and is planning on further body exploration.

Elena lives in Sarasota with her husband Alex and cat Vaska.

fax and mail order form

TOE-RRIFIC, a simple guide to creating healthy and beautiful feet

Please fill out the order form below and
    mail it to: **Toe-rrific, 4107 Duck Creek Way, Ellenton, FL 34222.**
    or fax it to: **512-857-6821**
For online orders please go to **www.toerrific.com**

Please send _____ copy(s) of TOE-RRIFIC

Name: _____

Address: _____

City: _____ State _____ Zip _____

Telephone: _____ Fax: _____

E-mail: _____

Cost of book $24.95   _____

Add 7% for books shipped
to Florida ($1.40 per book)   + _____

Please add shipping and handling in U.S.:
If purchasing one book, please
add $4.95 shipping/handling.*   + _____
If purchasing two or more books, add $0.

Total: = _____

Make check payable to "Happy Women Publishing"
or use credit card.

Card Type: ___ Visa   ___ MasterCard
                ___ Discover   ___ American Express

Card Number: _____ Exp. date: _____

Name on Card: _____

Cardholder's Address
/if different from above/ _____

Authorized Signature: _____

* We will ship your order the standard book rate. Average order turnaround is two to seven business days.

For quicker shipping methods or bulk purchase information, please go to www.toerrific.com or call 941-729-7141.

bright ideas

drop us a line...

Use this back side of the Order Form to let us know how your Toe-rrific designs came out. Please send us your ideas for new tools, new designs and tips for our next book. We can't wait to see how beautiful you are.

Our Address: Toe-rrific, 4107 Duck Creek Way, Ellenton, FL 34222.

Name _____

Address _____

Phone _____

Email _____

My Ideas: _____

_____

_____

_____

_____

My New Design Ideas:

We hope you had as much fun with this book as we did creating it. This was a great experience and we are looking forward producing many more exciting books that will help you feel as beautiful as you really are.

Thanks,

Elena and Cathleen

you can also look us up at our website at www.toerrific.com

We are adding new designs to our website and putting up new ideas contributed by all of you. Visit us on-line and share your toe-rrific ideas.